Maths all around you

STATISTICS

Rob Colson

WAYLAND

First published in Great Britain
in 2025 by Wayland
Copyright © Hodder and Stoughton Limited, 2025
All rights reserved

Series editor: Amy Pimperton
Designed and edited by Tall Tree Ltd
Consultant: Jim Newall
Artist: Joseph Wilkins/Beehive Art Agency

HB ISBN: 978 1 5263 2053 7
PB ISBN: 978 1 5263 2054 4

Wayland
An imprint of Hachette Children's Group
Part of Hodder and Stoughton
Carmelite House
50 Victoria Embankment
London EC4Y 0DZ

An Hachette UK Company
www.hachette.co.uk
www.hachettechildrens.co.uk

The authorised representative in the EEA is Hachette Ireland, 8 Castlecourt Centre, Dublin 15, D15 XTP3, Ireland (email: info@hbgi.ie)

Printed and bound in China

Picture Credits
FC-front cover, BC-back cover, t-top, b-bottom, l-left, r-right, c-centre
5b psmirnou/Shutterstock, 7tr Sabelskaya/Shutterstock, 8tl WinWin artlab/Shutterstock, 12 Andrew Krasovitckii/Shutterstock, 15 chekart/Shutterstock, 21t Morphart Creation/Shutterstock, 26 Macrovector/Shutterstock, 33t Iconic Bestiary/Shutterstock, 33b Puwadon Sang/Shutterstock, 35tl elenabsl/Shutterstock, 35tr hvostik/Shutterstock, 36–37t Lecter/Shutterstock, 39t Ilya koushik/Shutterstock, 39br Anatolir/Shutterstock, 40tl Tribalium/Shutterstock

Every attempt has been made to clear copyright. Should there be any inadvertent omission, please apply to the publisher for rectification.

CONTENTS

4 Statistics and data
6 What's the mean?
8 Counting in tallies
10 Dot plots
12 Counting in pictures
14 Bar charts
16 Pie charts
18 Conversion charts
20 Counting people
22 Time graphs
24 Changes in the weather
26 Climate change
28 Budgeting money
30 Comparing statistics
32 Timetables
34 Keeping fit
36 Sports tables
38 Measuring performance
40 Food statistics
42 Holiday statistics
44 Quiz
47 Answers
48 Index

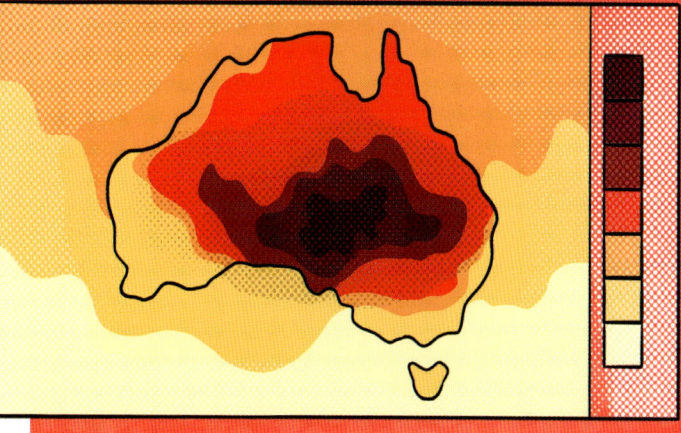

Statistics and data

Statistics is the part of maths that deals with data. Statisticians collect data and use it to understand the world around us.

What is data?

Data is a collection of facts. The facts might be numbers, words, measurements or observations.

Discrete data involves counting the quantity of things. The data can only take whole number values. For example, it might be the number of students in a class.

Continuous data involves measuring the size of something. It can take any value within a range, including fractions. For example, it might be the heights of students in a class.

Discrete data	Continuous data
Number of students in a class	Weight of a breed of dog
Shoe size	Height of classmates
Type of transport taken to school	Distance from home to school
Goals scored in football match	Time in a 100 metre race

Try this!
Throughout the book, there are puzzles for you to solve. Keep a pencil and notebook handy to write your answers in.

Analysing data

Once data has been collected, you need maths to analyse it. This means calculating values such as the mean (average). Data is also represented using graphs, which make it easier to spot patterns. The graph below shows how the number of electric cars in the world grew rapidly over a 10-year period.

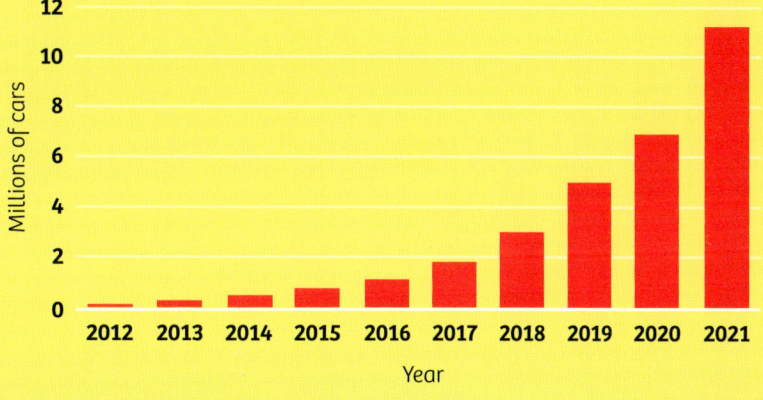

Data around us

Doctors collect data about their patients such as blood pressure and weight. The data helps doctors to monitor changes in the patients' health over time.

Governments keep data on where people live. They use the data to work out who is allowed to vote in elections.

Music platforms collect data about the songs people listen to. They use the data to suggest new songs that people might like.

What's the mean?

The mean is a calculation of the average value of a set of numbers.

Calculating the mean

To calculate the mean of a set of numbers, add up all the numbers then divide by how many numbers you have. For example, what is the average of the four numbers **2, 7, 11** and **12**?

First, add the numbers up: **2 + 7 + 11 + 12 = 32**. Then divide by how many numbers there are: **32 ÷ 4 = 8**

Averages around us

A baseball batter's batting average is the total number of 'hits' divided by the number of times 'at bat'. An average of 0.250, or one quarter, means that a batter has on average one hit every four times at bat.

Sometimes, no single piece of data is exactly the mean. For example, the average number of aces in a set of men's tennis is 2.5, but nobody can hit half an ace!

Try this!

Here are the heights of six children in a class:

Feng 134 cm	Noah 132 cm	Aadan 136 cm
Clare 143 cm	Abeda 145 cm	Leon 138 cm

One student has exactly the mean height. Who is it?

What is the mean height of the people who live in your home?

Answers on page 47

Counting in tallies

Tally marks are a quick way to record the numbers of something when collecting data.

Tallies are counted in groups of five. The first four marks are vertical, while the fifth mark is a diagonal line that goes across the other four lines. This is known as the five bar gate.

1 2 3 4 5 6 7 8 9 10

A tally of 27 looks like this:

Chinese tallies

In China, tallies of five are often written by forming the character 正 (zheng), meaning 'upright'. They are written in this sequence:

一 丁 下 正 正

1 2 3 4 5

A tally of 27 looks like this:

正 正 正 正 正 丁

Tukey tallies

American statistician John Tukey (1915–2000) used a system of dots and lines to count in tallies of ten. **Try writing tallies in different systems. Which one do you find the easiest to use?**

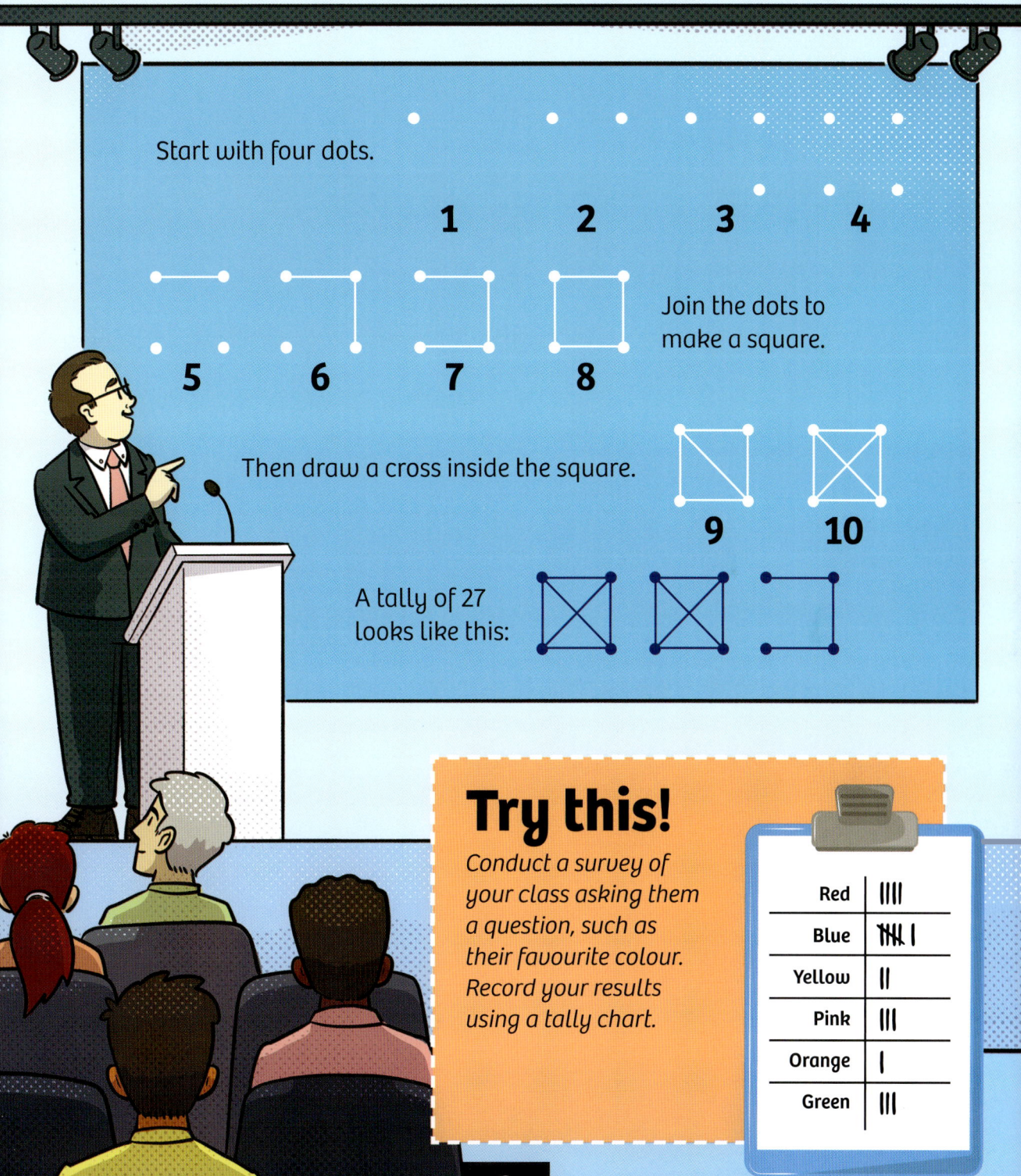

Start with four dots.

1 2 3 4

Join the dots to make a square.

5 6 7 8

Then draw a cross inside the square.

9 10

A tally of 27 looks like this:

Try this!

Conduct a survey of your class asking them a question, such as their favourite colour. Record your results using a tally chart.

Colour	Tally
Red	IIII
Blue	𝍦 I
Yellow	II
Pink	III
Orange	I
Green	III

Dot plots

Dot plots are a simple way to display data using stacks of dots. They are good to use when you are representing small amounts of data.

This data set shows the number of books a class read on their summer holidays.

Books read	0	1	2	3	4	5	6	7	8
Number of students	1	5	6	8	2	1	0	1	1

To turn this data into a dot plot, first you need to choose your horizontal scale. In this case, the scale shows the number of books read. It goes from the smallest value (0) to the largest value (8).

Now, stack the number of students above each value for books read, with one dot representing one student. Make the dots the same size and evenly spaced.

Looking at the dot plot, it is easy to see that most students read between 1 and 3 books, but some read many more.

Dot plots around us

Election results are often shown using dot plots. Each dot represents a seat in parliament. The chart below shows the results of the 2020 election in the Korea Republic.

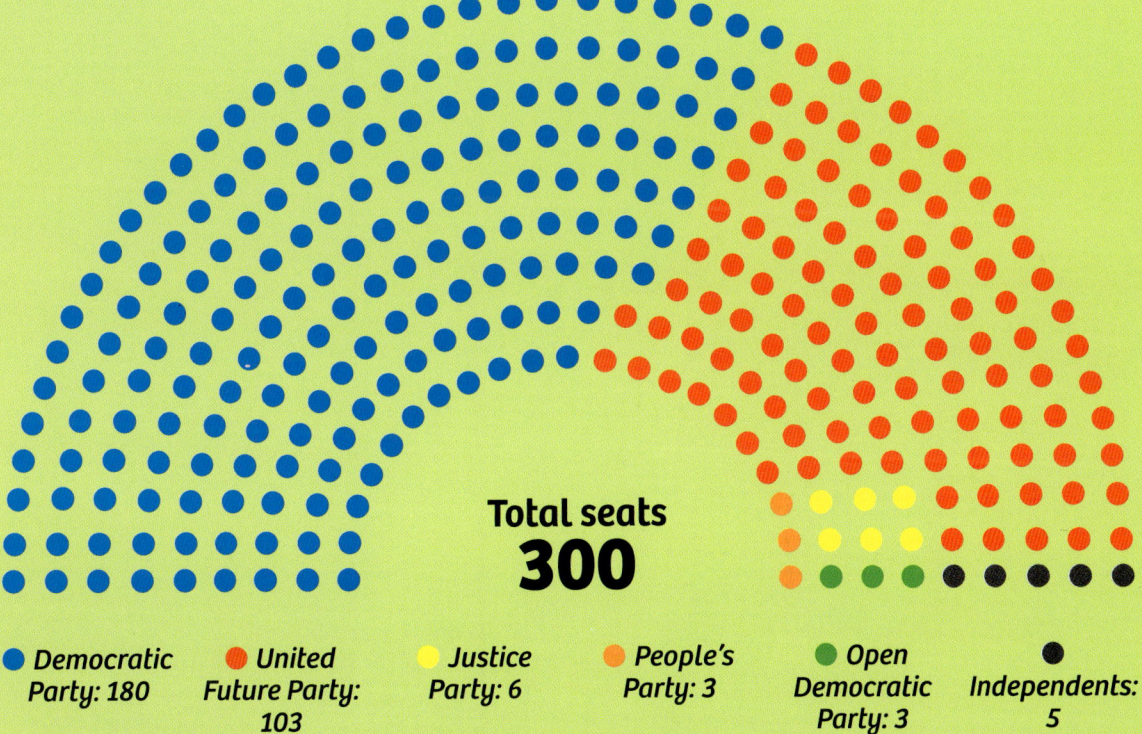

- Democratic Party: 180
- United Future Party: 103
- Justice Party: 6
- People's Party: 3
- Open Democratic Party: 3
- Independents: 5

Total seats **300**

In order to form a government, a party needs a majority of the seats, which is 151 seats or more. The Democratic Party formed the new government.

Try this!

Take the results of a survey that you have recorded on a tally chart and turn the results into a dot plot. You could use the survey you conducted for the activity on page 7.

Measure your horizontal line to make sure that each stack of dots is equally spaced. If you have made a survey of favourite colours, use those colours for the dots.

Counting in pictures

Pictograms are charts that use symbols to represent data. Always remember to read the key for a pictogram to understand what the symbols mean.

Tally charts can be turned into pictograms. Below is a pictogram showing a class's favourite animals after a school zoo visit.

Pictograms around us

Film critics often use stars to show how good they think a film is.

Sometimes the rating is an average score from many different critics, so you can have half-stars.

This pictogram shows how many customers bought coffee each day in a shop during the course of a week. One coffee cup stands for ten customers. Half a cup is five customers. For example, on Friday, 50 people bought coffee.

How many people bought coffee on Tuesday?

Try this!

This pictogram shows a class's favourite pizza toppings.

a) How many children prefer pepperoni?
b) Do more children prefer seafood and meat or vegetables?
c) If you change the key so that a whole pizza represents 2 children, how many pizza symbols will be needed for mushrooms?

Pepperoni

Mushrooms *Peppers*

Seafood *Pineapple*

Key: 1 pizza = 4 children

Answers on page 47

Bar charts

Bar charts show the relative sizes of things in a way that is easy to look at.

Data in a table can be turned into a bar chart. This makes it much easier to see which values are the largest and smallest.

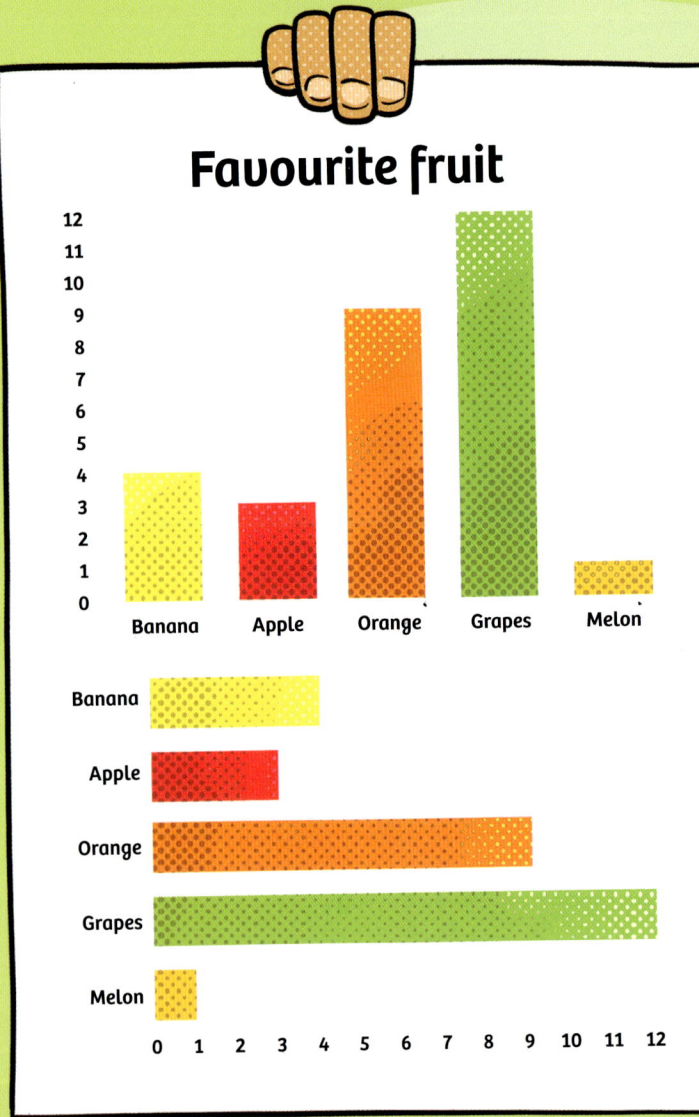

A bar chart can be shown with the bars running vertically or horizontally.

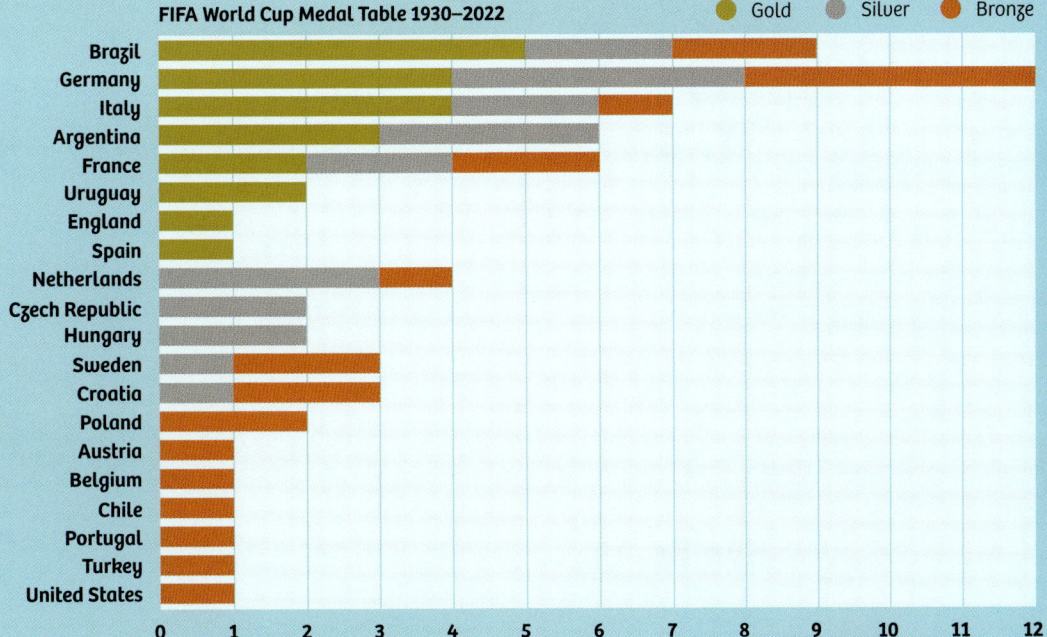

Bar charts around us

Sometimes it is useful to split each bar in a bar chart into different colours to show the different parts of the total. This is called a stacked bar chart.

The bar chart above shows countries that have won gold (1st), silver (2nd) or bronze (3rd) medals at the FIFA World Cup up to 2022. The gold and silver are awarded to the winner and loser of the final, while the bronze is awarded to the winner of the 3rd/4th place play-off match.

Try this!

Look at the bar chart at the top and answer the following questions.

1. Which country has won the World Cup the most times?
2. How many countries have made the final of the World Cup?
3. Which country has made the final three times but lost on each occasion?

Answers on page 47

Pie Charts

A pie chart shows statistics as sectors of a circle.
The sectors look like slices of a pie.

How to make a pie chart

First, write down your statistics in a table. For example, this table shows the favourite films of a class:

Comedy	Action	Romance	SciFi	Total
10	8	7	5	30

Next, divide each value by the total to produce fractions.

Comedy	Action	Romance	SciFi	Total
10	8	7	5	30
$\frac{10}{30}$	$\frac{8}{30}$	$\frac{7}{30}$	$\frac{5}{30}$	

Now you need to work out the angle for each sector. A full circle has 360°, so you multiply each fraction by 360.

Comedy	Action	Romance	SciFi	Total
10	8	7	5	30
$\frac{10}{30}$	$\frac{8}{30}$	$\frac{7}{30}$	$\frac{5}{30}$	
$\frac{10}{30} \times 360° = 120°$	$\frac{8}{30} \times 360° = 96°$	$\frac{7}{30} \times 360° = 84°$	$\frac{5}{30} \times 360° = 60°$	

Now it is time to draw your pie chart. Using a pair of compasses, draw a circle. Using a protractor, carefully measure the degrees of each sector and draw the lines from the centre. Colour each sector and give it a name.

Pie charts around us

People often use pie charts when they are making presentations to large groups. Displaying a colourful pie chart on a screen is an easy way to help everyone to understand the information. This pie chart shows a clothes shop's monthly sales of different products. However, pie charts only show the relative sizes of the sales. To show exactly what number each sector represents, you need to add numbers to the chart.

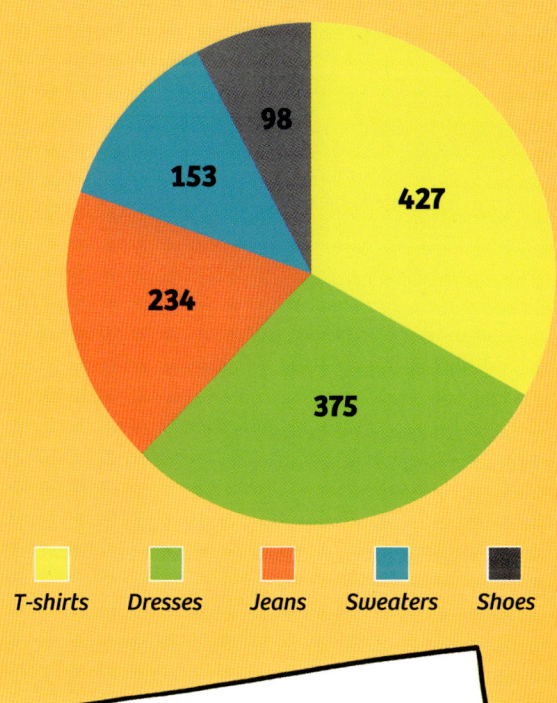

T-shirts   Dresses   Jeans   Sweaters   Shoes

Try this!

Take a look at the following pie chart showing the favourite sports of 20 children in a class, then answer the questions below.

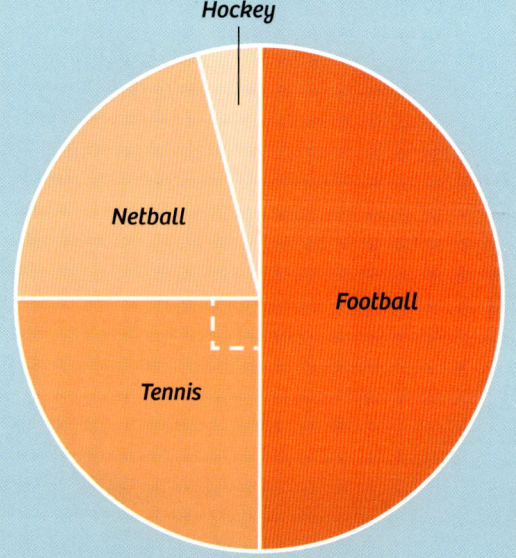

a) What is the angle marked in the Tennis sector? (Hint: Work out what fraction of the total prefer tennis, then multiply by 360°.)
b) What fraction of children prefer football?
c) How many children prefer netball?

Answers on page 47

Conversion graphs

Conversion graphs are straight lines that allow you to compare two different units and convert one to the other.

This conversion graph compares miles to kilometres.

Maddie and Joshua's cycle ride to school is 2 miles. **How many kilometres is the cycle ride?**

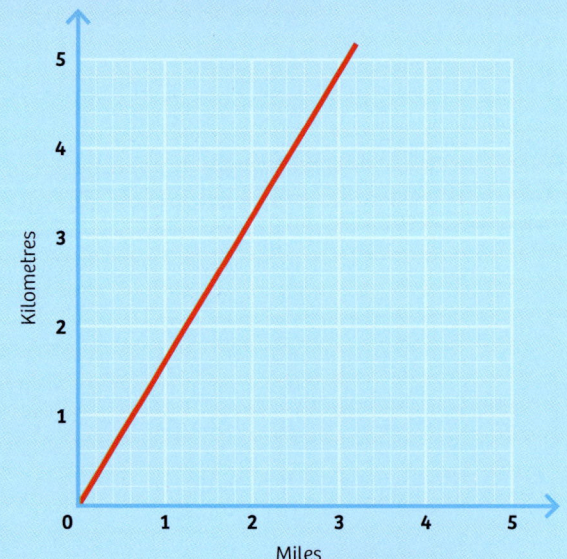

This conversion graph compares the US dollar to the Chinese Yuan. **If a toy car costs US$9, how much does it cost in Yuan?**

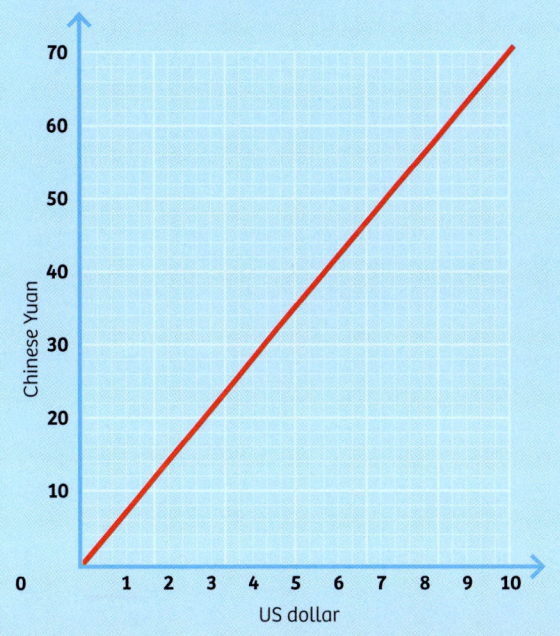

This conversion graph compares pounds to kilogrammes. **If a cat weighs 4.5 kilogrammes, how much does it weigh in pounds?**

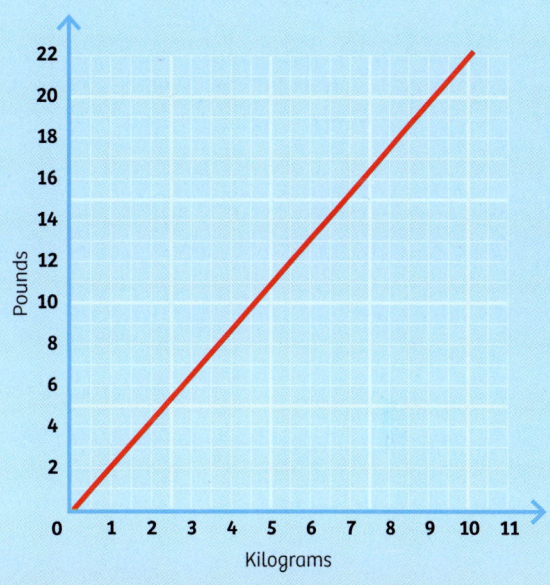

Conversion graphs around us

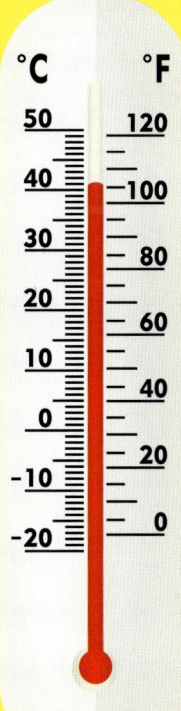

Many thermometers show temperature in both the Celsius and Fahrenheit scales. On the thermometer to the left, the scales are shown vertically. This can be changed to a conversion graph by placing degrees Celsius along a horizontal axis. Negative numbers are also needed.

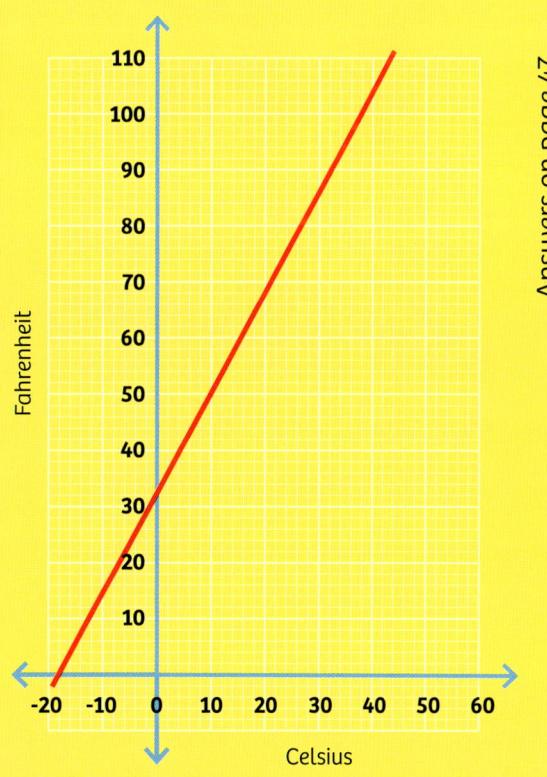

Answers on page 47

Counting people

Governments gather statistics about the people in a country in censuses. They record data such as births and deaths, sex, age and education level. This helps them to plan public services.

Taking a census

Many countries carry out a census of the whole population every ten years. This produces an up-to-date record of how the population has changed. According to national censuses, the three largest countries in the world by population are China, India and the USA.

China

2020	**1,412 million (1.412 billion)**
2010	**1,340 million**
2000	**1,295 million**
1990	**1,134 million**

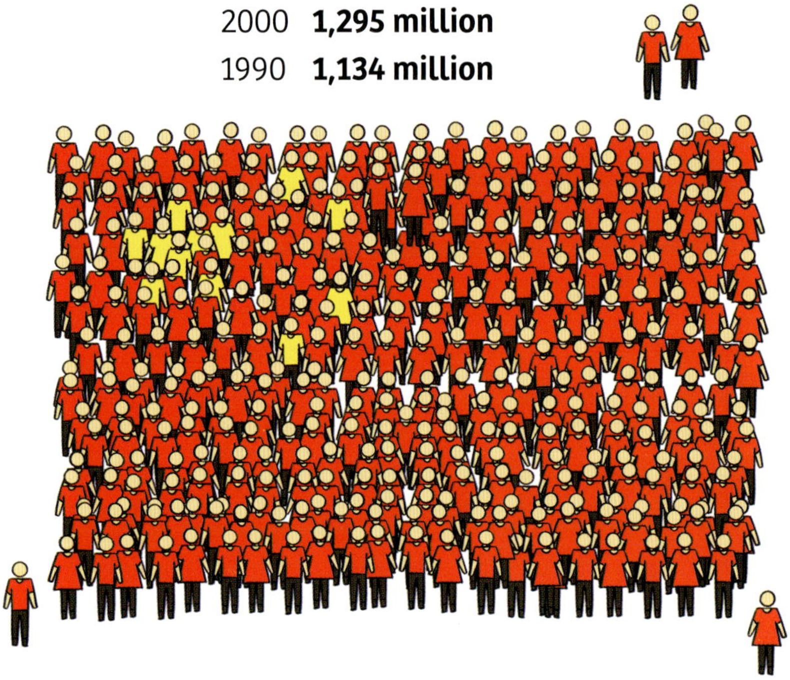

India

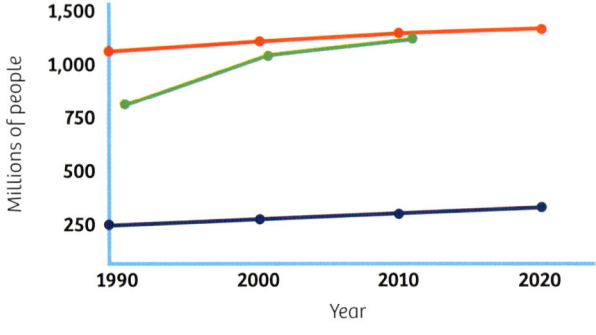

By drawing these results on a graph, you can see that India's population has grown quickly, while the populations of of China and the USA have grown more slowly.

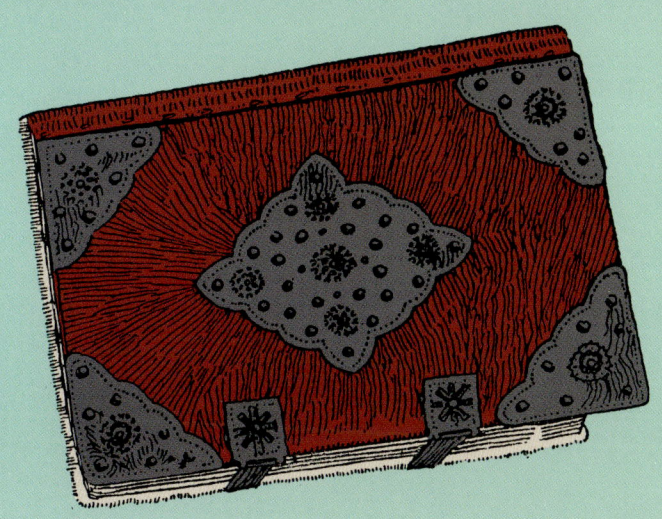

The Domesday Book

One of the first ever national censuses was carried out in England in the year 1086. King William I had come to power a few years earlier. He carried out the census in order to find out how much tax he was owed by his new subjects!

2021	**Delayed to 2024**
2011	**1,210 million**
2001	**1,029 million**
1991	**839 million**

USA

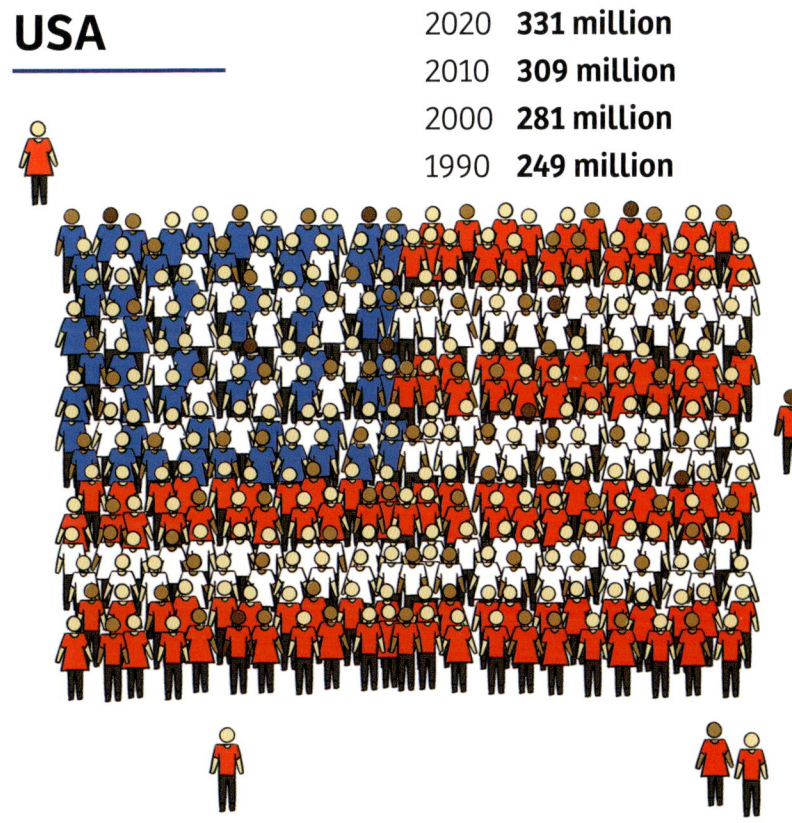

2020	**331 million**
2010	**309 million**
2000	**281 million**
1990	**249 million**

Try this!

The results of most censuses are published on the Internet. **Can you find the census data on your town or state? How has the population changed over time?**

Time graphs

Time graphs show how a value has changed over time. Time is usually plotted along a horizontal line, with the other value, such as distance or temperature, on a vertical line. Time graphs make it easy to spot patterns.

This time-distance line graph shows Hannah's walk to school. The line is flat for five minutes because Hannah stopped to talk to her friend! Realising she was late, she ran the rest of the way!

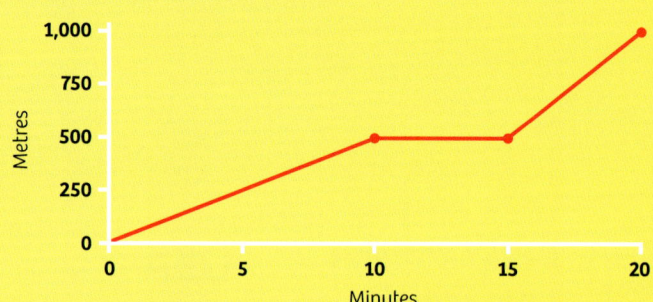

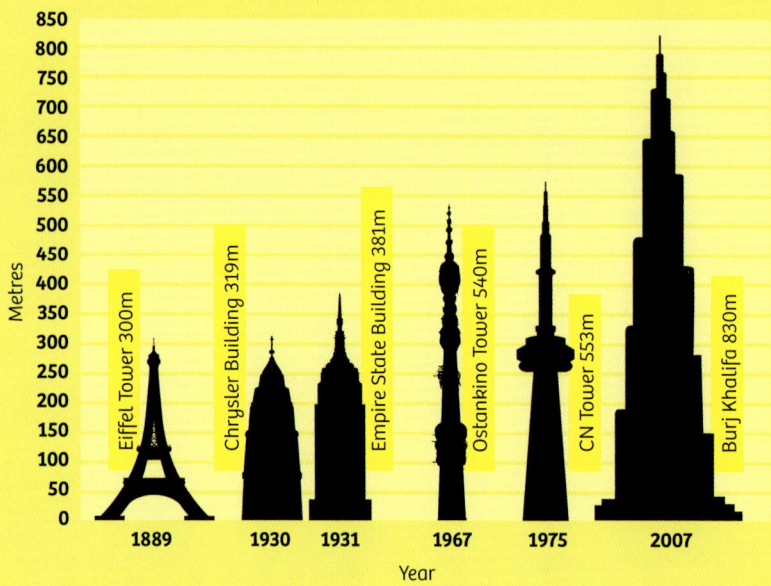

Time graphs can also show how records have developed over time. Here is a time-height graph showing how the tallest structure in the world has changed over time.

This time graph shows how the 100 metres world record has changed over time:

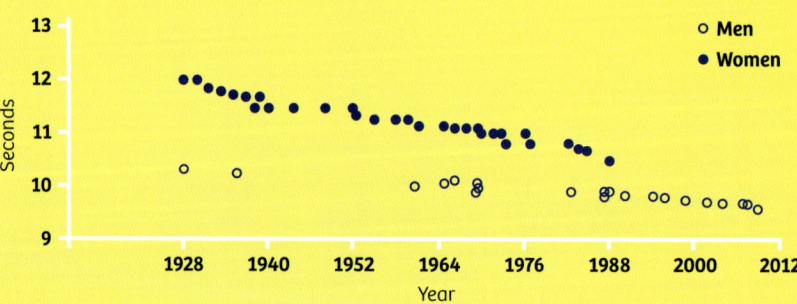

The times of the records in seconds are recorded on the vertical axis. **Which record has improved the most over the last 100 years – the men's or the women's?**

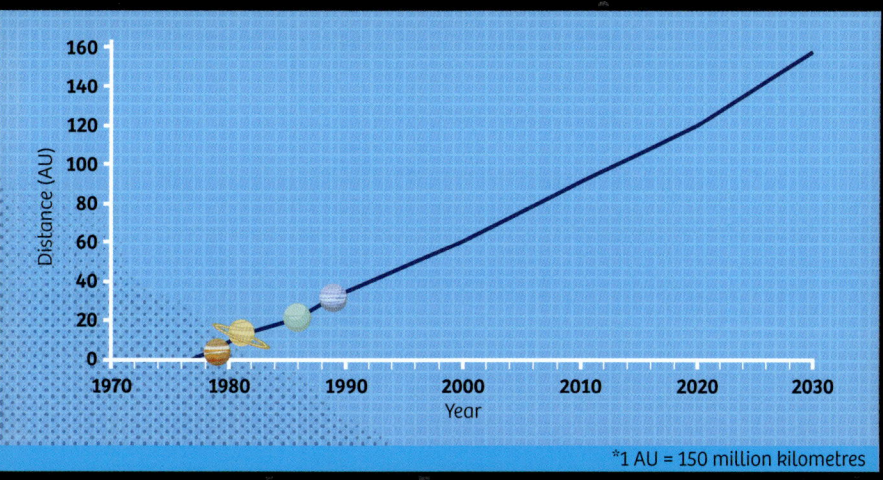

Moving through space

The Voyager 2 space probe was launched into space in 1977. This time-distance graph shows how far it has travelled since then and all the planets it has passed along the way. It also shows where Voyager 2 will be in the year 2030.

Try this!

This time-distance graph shows how far away from home Kai is throughout the day. His school is 2 km from home. The swimming pool is 0.5 km further away. Kai's friend Niall's house is 1 km from school on Niall's way home. Can you tell the story of Kai's day?

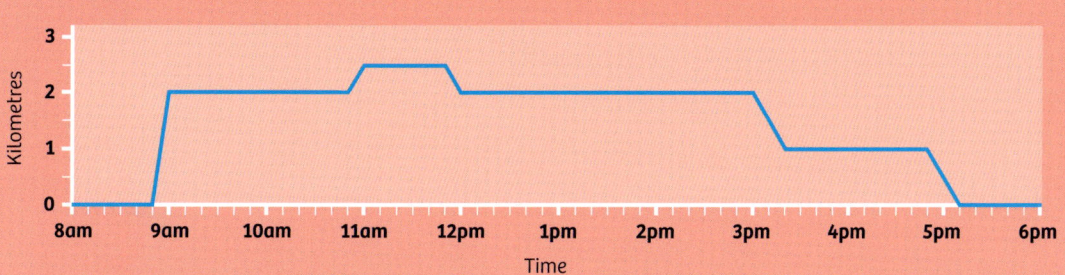

How do you think Kai got to school? Did he walk or take the bus? [Hint: work out how far he travelled and how long it took him. ***Do you think this is possible on foot?***] When did Kai go swimming? What time did Kai arrive at Niall's house?

Answers on page 47

Changes in the weather

Changes in the weather are often shown using time graphs.

Time	Temperature (°C)
12am	6
2am	5
4am	3
6am	2
8am	5
10am	9
12pm	12
2pm	14
4pm	14
6pm	13
8pm	10
10pm	8

Hot or cold?

By plotting temperature against time, you can see clearly how the temperature drops at night and rises during the day.

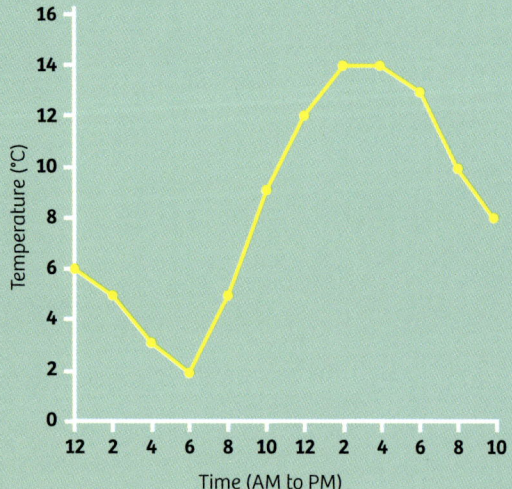

The temperature is often lowest around dawn and highest in the early afternoon. From looking at the time graph, when do you think dawn occurred?

Changing tides

The times and heights of the ocean tides change from day to day. A tide table tells you when high tide and low tide will occur each day. To the right is a tide table for four days of a week.

Below are these tides plotted as points on a time graph. Lines between the points make it easier to see how the tides go up and down.

TUESDAY		WEDNESDAY	
Time	Metres	Time	Metres
5:10am	0.9	5:56am	0.9
11:26am	5.8	12:12pm	5.8
5:42pm	0.7	6:30pm	0.7
11:54pm	5.6		

THURSDAY		FRIDAY	
Time	Metres	Time	Metres
12:43am	5.5	1:35am	5.3
6:45am	1.0	7:33am	1.2
1:01pm	5.7	1:53pm	5.6
7:20pm	0.8	8:15pm	0.9

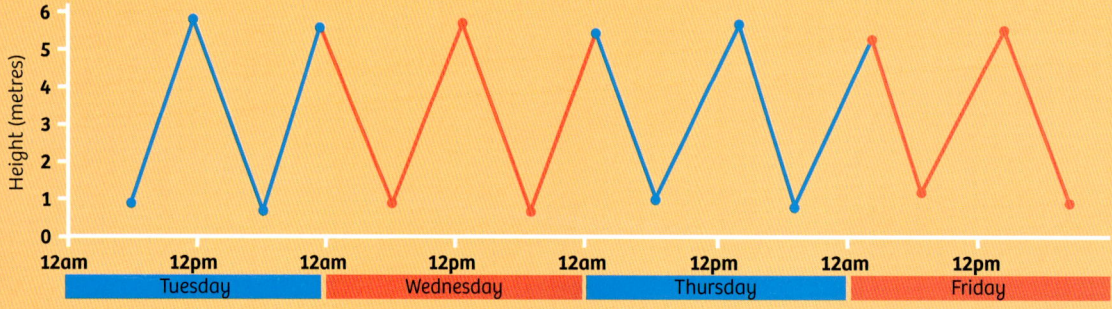

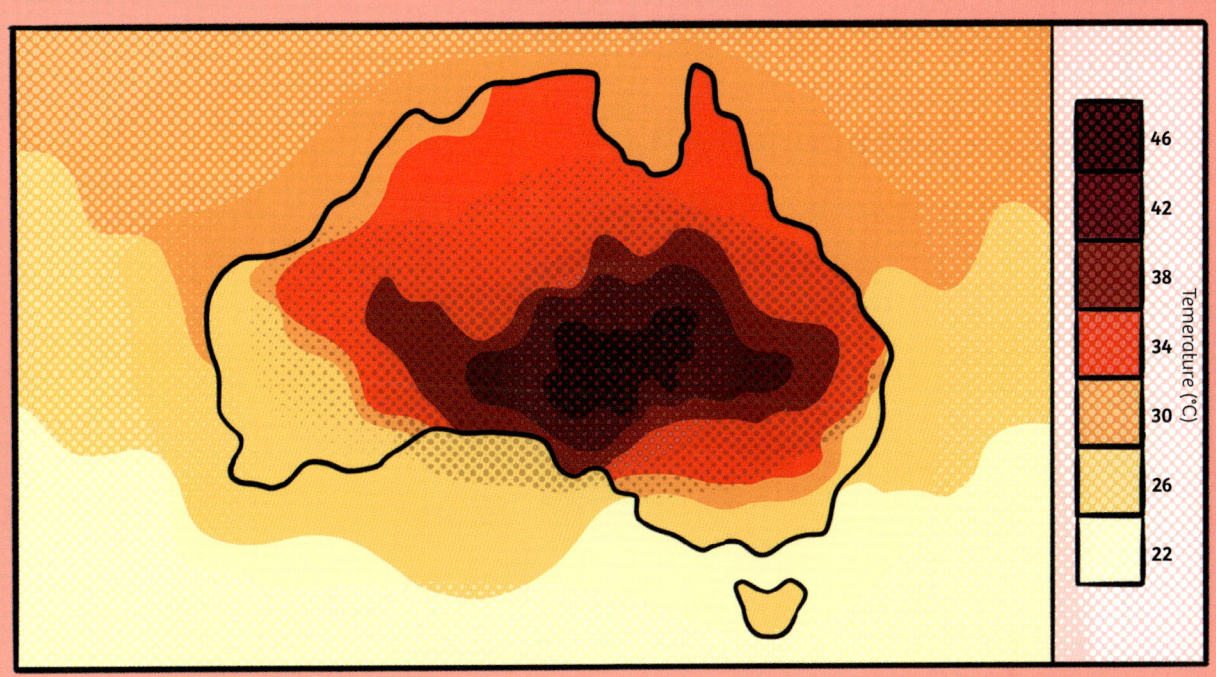

Weather data around us

Scientists display weather data on coloured maps to show how statistics such as temperature vary across an area of the world. A key next to the map shows what the colours mean.

The map above was made by scientists in Australia to show the temperature on the hottest day during a record-breaking summer heat wave. They had to add a new colour to their key (purple) to show record-high temperatures of more than 52°C!

Climate change

Scientists gather statistics about the world's climate to show that the planet is warming. They present their results in graphs to inform us about climate change and help us to understand what we can do to stop it.

The Hockey Stick

In the 1990s, scientists produced a graph showing how the average temperature on Earth has changed over the last 1,000 years. The graph is shaped like a hockey stick – it is a relatively flat line up to the year 1900, and then shows a steady increase through the 20th century.

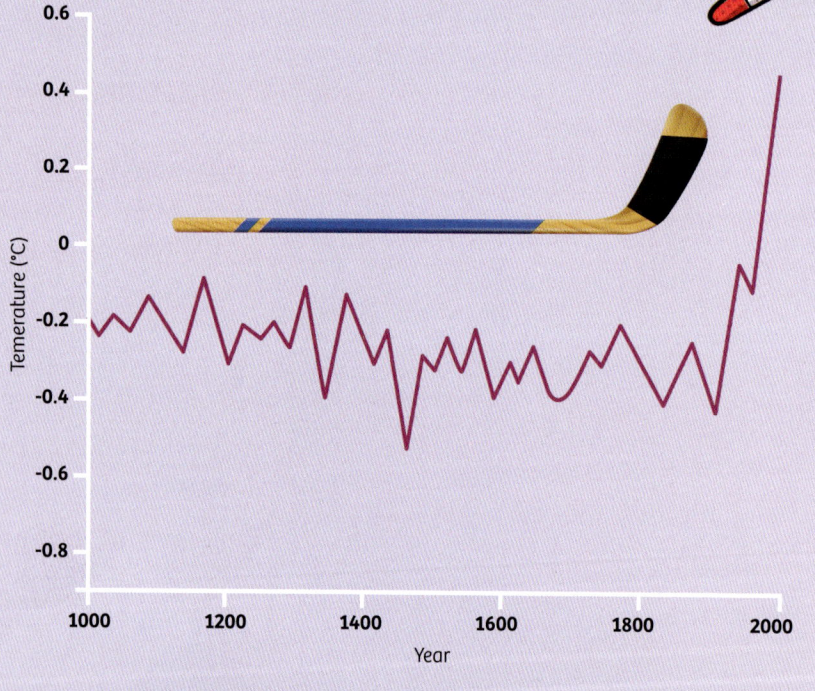

The rise in Earth's temperature is making extreme weather events such as storms, wildfires and droughts much more common. By keeping the rise in temperature below 1.5°C, we can help to stop the worst effects of climate change.

Greenhouse gases

Our climate is warming because we are putting gases known as greenhouse gases into the atmosphere. These gases stop heat from escaping into space.

To the right are the greenhouse gases produced by human activity in a pie chart.

To stop global warming, we need to reduce the amount of carbon dioxide we are producing. The pie chart below shows the human sources of carbon dioxide.

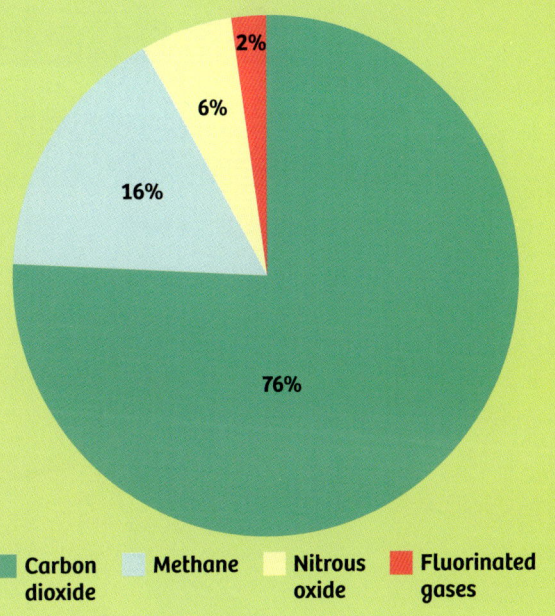

- Carbon dioxide
- Methane
- Nitrous oxide
- Fluorinated gases

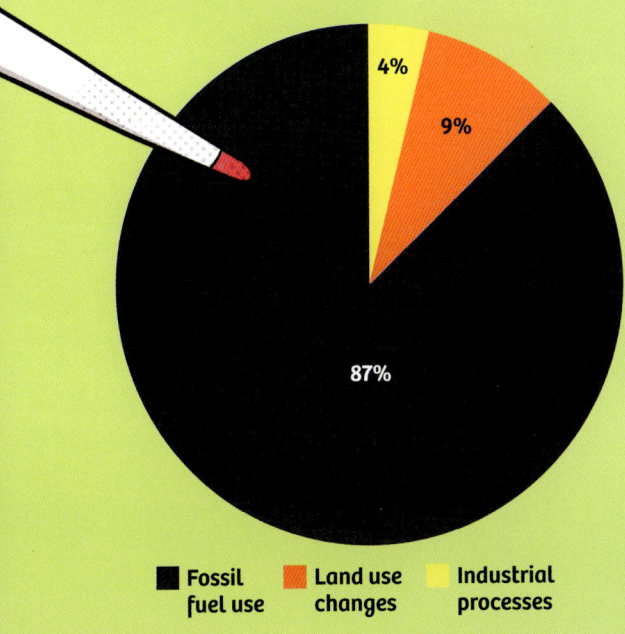

- Fossil fuel use
- Land use changes
- Industrial processes

Fossil fuels are fuels such as oil, coal and natural gas, which produce carbon dioxide when they burn. Over the next few years, countries have committed to reducing their use of fossil fuels. We will do this by generating more electricity using clean sources such as wind or solar power, by changing to electric cars, and also by using electric devices more efficiently.

Budgeting money

Budgets are ways to manage your money. You have a maximum amount you can afford to spend, and you have to decide both what you need to buy and what you don't!

Your parents or carers are planning a birthday party for you and seven of your friends. They've asked you to help them to plan the budget for the party. What will you choose to have?

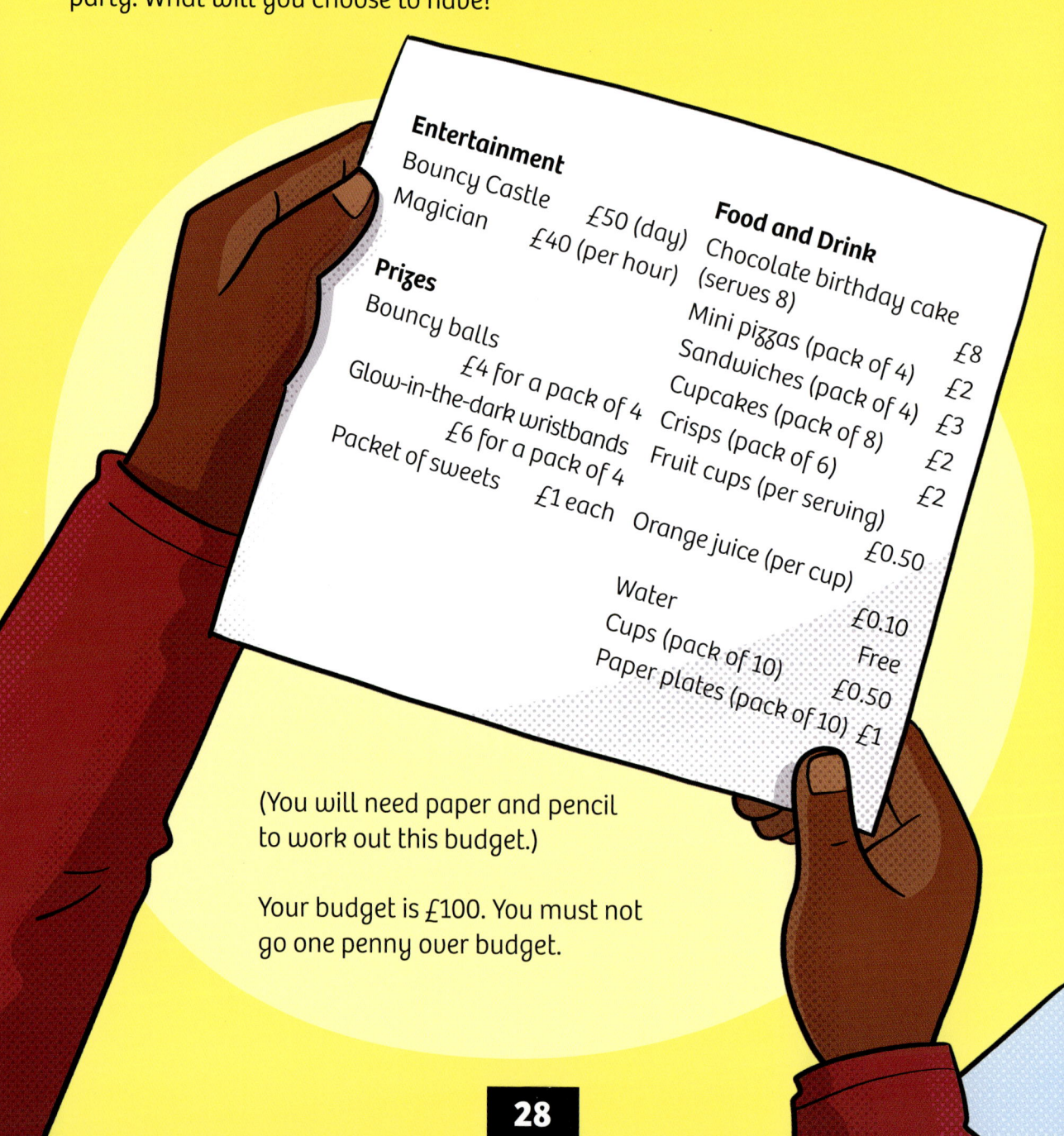

Entertainment
Bouncy Castle £50 (day)
Magician £40 (per hour)

Prizes
Bouncy balls £4 for a pack of 4
Glow-in-the-dark wristbands £6 for a pack of 4
Packet of sweets £1 each

Food and Drink
Chocolate birthday cake (serves 8) £8
Mini pizzas (pack of 4) £2
Sandwiches (pack of 4) £3
Cupcakes (pack of 8) £2
Crisps (pack of 6) £2
Fruit cups (per serving) £0.50
Orange juice (per cup) £0.10
Water Free
Cups (pack of 10) £0.50
Paper plates (pack of 10) £1

(You will need paper and pencil to work out this budget.)

Your budget is £100. You must not go one penny over budget.

When planning your budget, make sure you have everything covered. There needs to be entertainment, plenty to eat and drink, and prizes for the games you play.

Don't just choose your favourites — there should be something for everyone!

Don't blow your whole budget on one thing!

Comparing statistics

When you compare sets of statistics, it's important to make sure that you are making a fair comparison.

What's the range?

Sometimes the mean does not give a complete picture of a set of data. Often, you also need the range, which is the difference between the largest number and the smallest number.

The table below shows Ai and Katie's ten times (in seconds) in the 100 metres freestyle swimming race across a season.

Ai	61	63	64	65	63	67	66	64	65	62
Katie	68	60	69	64	61	63	61	70	62	60

Ai's average time = $\frac{640}{10}$ = **64 seconds**

Katie's average time = $\frac{638}{10}$ = **63.8 seconds**

The range of Ai's times = **67 – 61 = 6 seconds**
The range of Katie's times = **70 – 60 = 10 seconds**

Katie has a slightly better average time, but Ai has a much smaller range. This means that Ai is a more consistent swimmer. Who would you pick for your team?

Jump like a flea

A flea can jump up 20 centimetres into the air. If you try jumping, you will probably find that you can jump as high as a flea.

But 20 centimetres is **150 times** a flea's height. Adjusting for size, that's like you jumping more than 200 metres into the air, or clean over the Great Pyramid of Giza!

Comparing statistics around us

When comparing how rich a country is, statisticians divide the country's total wealth (known as GDP) by the number of people who live there. This produces a figure called GDP per capita and allows us to compare the wealth of countries of very different sizes.

The GDP of Norway is **US$ 320 billion**.

The GDP of India is **US$ 3.2 trillion**. That's ten times larger than the GDP of Norway.

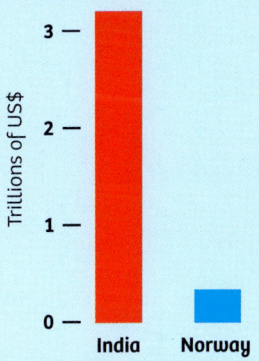

Norway has a population of **5.4 million**. Its GDP per capita is **US$ 320 billion ÷ 5.4 million = US$ 59,000**.

India has a population of **1.4 billion**. Its GDP per capita is **US$ 3.2 trillion ÷ 1.4 billion = US$ 2,300**.

While Norway is a much smaller country than India, it is a richer country, with more than 25 times as much wealth per person.

Try this!

What is the GDP per capita of the country you live in?

Timetables

A timetable is a way of showing information that says when something will happen.

A bus timetable shows the time a bus will arrive at each bus stop. Below is the school bus timetable for Oak Tree School.

School Bus

Forest Hill	7:50
Newton	8:05
Arke Ville	8:10
Old Town	8:15
Oak Tree School	8:30

Timetables can be colour-coded to make them easier to read. For example, this swimming pool timetable shows family swim in blue and adult-only in brown.

ADULT SWIM	6:30am – 11:30am
POOL CLOSED	11:30am – 12pm
FAMILY SWIM	12pm – 1:30pm
POOL CLOSED	1:30pm – 2pm
FAMILY SWIM	2pm – 3:30pm
ADULT SWIM	3:30pm – 4:30pm
FAMILY SWIM	4:30pm – 6pm
ADULT SWIM	6pm – 9pm

Pupils who live in Old Town have 25 minutes longer to get ready for school than pupils from Forest Hill!

Timetables around us

Schools use maths to create exam timetables. They need to space out the exams so that all the students have time to study. Computer programs help schools to choose the best timetable.

Try this!

Can you help complete this school timetable? The number of classes per week need to be as set out to the right (two classes of the same subject are not allowed on the same day).

Maths	4 classes
English	4 classes
Geography	2 classes
Science	4 classes
Music	1 class
Coding	1 class
Sport	4 classes

	Monday	Tuesday	Wednesday	Thursday	Friday
9:00–10:30	Maths	English	Science	Maths	Geography
Break					
11:00–12:00	English	Science	b)	Geography	Maths
Lunch time					
1:00–2:00	a)	Coding	Maths	English	Science
Break					
2:30–3:30	Sport	Music	Sport	Sport	c)

Answers on page 47

Keeping fit

Collecting statistics about our daily lives can help us to keep fit and be healthy.

BMI

A statistic known as BMI (Body Mass Index) is a number that helps you to find out if you are a healthy weight. BMI is calculated by dividing your weight in kilogrammes by your height in metres multiplied by itself. This gives a unit called kilogrammes per metre squared (kg/m²).

For example, if your weight is **50 kg** and your height is **1.5 metres**, your BMI = $\frac{50}{(1.5 \times 1.5)}$ = **22.2 kg/m²**.

What is your BMI?

Doctors calculate a patient's BMI to estimate whether they are a healthy weight. However, we all have different bodies, so doctors take account of other factors, in addition to BMI, to work out overall health.

Daily exercise

Most healthy children should aim to exercise for at least one hour every day. Playing games with your friends is a great way to exercise. You should regularly do activities such as running, cycling or swimming that raise your heart rate and leave you a little out of breath.

Add up all the periods of exercise you have during a typical day. Remember that even a few minutes playing counts towards your total.

Smart watches

Smart watches monitor your body throughout the day. They measure how many steps you have taken in the day and also keep track of your heart rate, blood pressure and sleep patterns. People with smart watches can set themselves daily goals for the number of steps they take to help them to stay healthy.

Do any of your activities leave you out of breath?

Try this!

Record your pulse and see how your heart rate increases when you exercise. You'll need a stopwatch, pencil and paper.

1. *First check your pulse at rest. Do this by holding two fingers over your wrist to feel the pulse. Count the number of beats in 15 seconds and multiply this number by 4 to give the number of beats per minute. For example, 20 beats in 15 seconds would be 80 beats per minute.*
2. *Run around outside or do star jumps continuously for one minute. Then immediately check your pulse.*
3. *Rest for one minute then check your pulse again.*

How long does it take for your heart rate to return to its resting rate?

Answers on page 47

Sports tables

League tables keep track of how sports teams are performing throughout a season.

Football Leagues

In the English Premier League, 20 teams play each other twice across the season, making 38 games in total. Three points are awarded for a win, one point for a draw and no points for a defeat. If teams are level on points, position is decided on goal difference (GD): number of goals scored (for) minus the number of goals conceded (against). This is how the top two looked before the final round of matches in the 2021–2022 season:

	P	W	D	L	Points	Goals for	Goals against
1. Manchester City	37	28	6	3	90	96	24
2. Liverpool	37	27	8	2	89	91	25

In a thrilling end to the season, both teams won their final matches, meaning that Manchester City won the league by just one point.

Baseball standings

In Major League Baseball (MLB), teams play 162 games per season. A baseball game always has a winner and a loser. The teams' standings are measured as a percentage. This is calculated as the number of wins divided by the number of games, multiplied by 100. The American League East finished like the table to the right in 2019.

	W	L	%
1. New York Yankees	103	59	63.6
2. Tampa Bay Rays	96	66	59.3
3. Boston Red Sox	84	78	50.9
4. Toronto Blue Jays	67	95	41.4
5. Baltimore Orioles	67	95	41.4

The New York Yankees won the most games. Their percentage wins = $\frac{103}{162} \times 100 = 63.6\%$

Try this!

In the FIFA Women's World Cup, the 32 teams are split into eight groups of four teams. The teams play matches against all the teams in their group. The top two teams from each group go through to the next round. Below is the state of Group F with one round of matches to go.

	P	W	D	L	Points	GD
France	2	1	1	0	4	+2
China	2	1	1	0	4	+1
Nigeria	2	1	0	1	3	+1
Canada	2	0	0	2	0	−4

The remaining matches are:
China vs Canada and **France vs Nigeria**

a) Which team cannot qualify for the next round?
b) Which teams just need to draw their final match to qualify?
c) If Nigeria draw with France, what does the result in the other match need to be for Nigeria to qualify?

Answers on page 47

Measuring performance

In addition to keeping track of a team's results, sports analysts use statistics to measure the performance of individual players.

Tracking players during play

Professional footballers often wear GPS trackers. These devices keep track of where the players are on the pitch during a game. At the end of the game, a computer uses the data to make a 'heat map' showing the areas of the pitch each player was in the most time.

The heat map on the right is for Argentinian forward Lionel Messi during one half of a game. Red shows the most time, and green the least. The heat map shows that he spent most of his time attacking the opposition, and that he played more on the right wing than on the left wing.

Yo-yo test

During training, player fitness is measured to make sure they are fit enough to play a game. One way to do this is to use a test called the yo-yo test. Players run between two markers placed 20 metres apart. They must run from one marker to the other in a certain time, then a beep sounds and they run back to their starting point.

20 metres

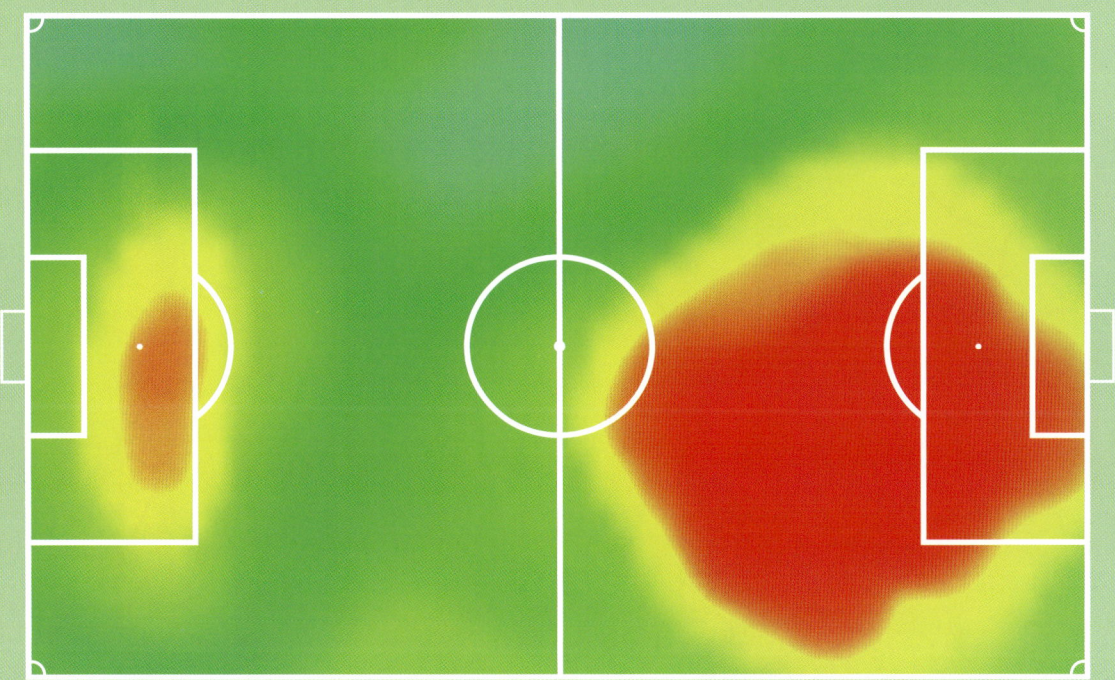

After a recovery period of 10 seconds, the test is repeated, but the time before the beep is reduced. Players keep going until they have missed two beeps.

Try this!

Measure your performance and compare it to your friends with a simple hula hoop game. Challenge your friends to see who can keep going the longest. Use a stopwatch to time yourselves and make a table showing your results. Do you improve with practice?

Food statistics

Food manufacturers include statistics about the nutrition of their food on the packaging.

Typically, the statistics on the label give the nutrition per 100 grammes.

This can of baked beans weighs 400 grammes, so you need to multiply all these figures by 4 to give the nutrition in a whole can. Energy is measured in a unit called kilocalories (kcal), which are often just called calories.

	Per 100g
Energy	100kcal
Fat	0.7g
Carbohydrate	13.5g
of which sugars	5.3g
Fibre	6.2g
Protein	4.6g
Salt	0.5g

How many full cans of baked beans would provide 2,000 calories?

Counting nutrition around us

Doctors give advice about how much of each nutrient we should be eating. Some people need to be very careful about what they eat. For example, diabetics need to know the amount of carbohydrate they eat so that they can keep the amount of sugar in their blood at a healthy level.

Daily vitamins and minerals

Vitamins and minerals are a range of nutrients that we need to eat in small quantities to stay healthy.

The daily recommended intake of Vitamin C for children aged 10 is 45 milligrammes (mg). That's 45 thousandths of a gramme. The maximum daily recommended intake of Vitamin C for children aged 10 is **1,200 mg**.

A 100 ml glass of orange juice contains about 50 mg of Vitamin C. You can safely drink a couple of glasses of orange juice in a day, but don't drink three litres! That would be 1,500 mg of Vitamin C, which could make you ill.

Eat a range of fruit and vegetables each day to make sure you get all your vitamins and minerals.

Try this!

You are making a meal for a diabetic friend, and it needs to contain no more than 40 grammes of carbohydrates. Choose three of the ingredients below to make a tasty meal.

	Carbohydrates (g)
Boiled egg	2
Baked potato	25
Portion of peas	20
Portion of carrots	10

Answers on page 47

Holiday statistics

People use charts of statistics to work out where to go on holiday. The charts tell them how likely it is to be warm and sunny or how often it rains.

Climographs are bar charts that show a region's climate data.

The climograph below shows the average rain and temperature each month on the island of Majorca. The bars show rainfall, with the scale on the right. The dots show temperature, with the scale on the left.

Summers in Majorca are hot and dry. Most people visit in July and August, when it is hottest, but some prefer the cooler temperatures in May and June. It is very dry from June to August.

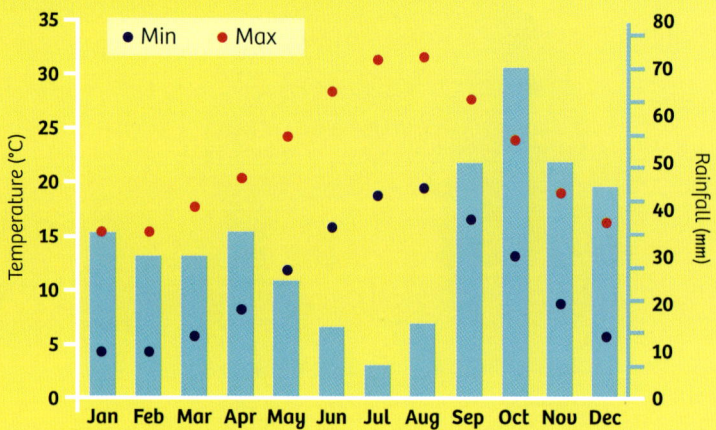

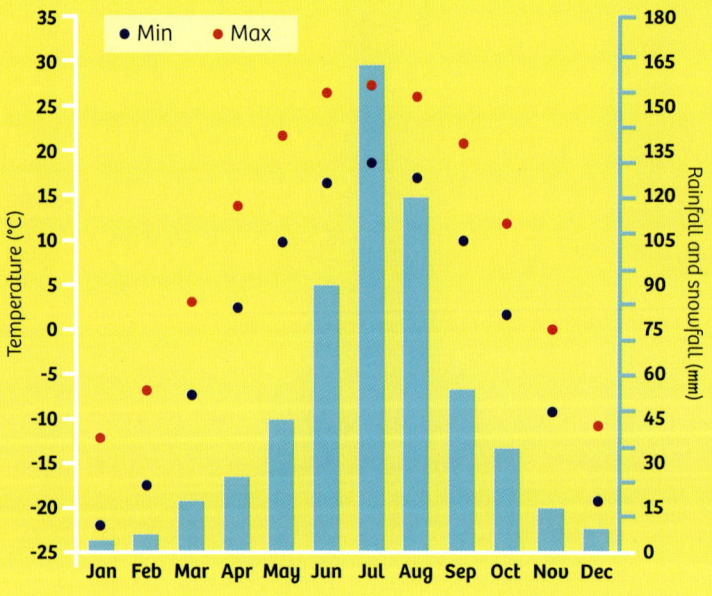

At a ski resort, you want it to be cold when you visit! To the left is the climograph for the Yabuli ski resort in Harbin, China.

It is cold enough to ski when the temperature is below 0°C for most of the day. **Which months should you visit if you want to go skiing?**

Answers on page 47

Popular destinations

Many people like to visit cities for their holidays. The bar chart below shows the top ten most visited cities in 2019. Hong Kong was the most visited city.

Other statistics that people use to measure the value of a holiday destination include the average sunshine hours and the number of rainy days.

When you go on holiday, what is the most important statistic you'd like to know about the places you visit?

Quiz

1 The number of aces hit in a tennis match is an example of:

a) Discrete data   **b)** Continuous data

2 Kai scored the following marks in weekly spelling tests: 16, 14, 17, 13. What was Kai's mean score in the four tests?

3 Which of the following statements is correct?

a) The mean average is the most common number in a set of numbers.
b) You calculate the mean average by adding up all the numbers then dividing by how many numbers you have.
c) The mean average is how many numbers you have in a set.

4 Which of the following Chinese tallies shows the number 18?

a)
b)
c)

5 What number does this Tukey tally mark show?

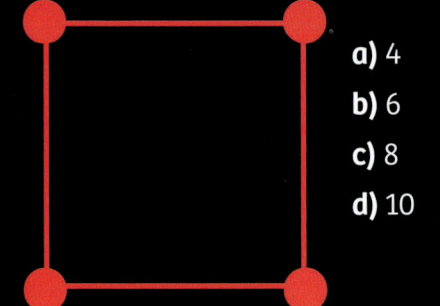

a) 4
b) 6
c) 8
d) 10

6 Look at the tally chart to the right showing the results of a survey of how students in travel to school, and answer the questions.

a) How many students ride a bicycle to school?
b) How many students take motorised transport to school?
c) How many students were surveyed in total?

7 This pictogram shows the number of ice creams sold in a day by flavour.

Chocolate Strawberry Vanilla Raspberry

Key: = 2 ice creams

a) Which ice cream flavour was the most popular and how many did it sell?
b) How many vanilla ice creams were sold?
c) How many ice creams were sold in total?

8 Which of the following bar charts correctly shows this weather data?

Days of snow
December 3   January 6   February 11   March 2

9 Which of the following pie charts correctly shows this data?

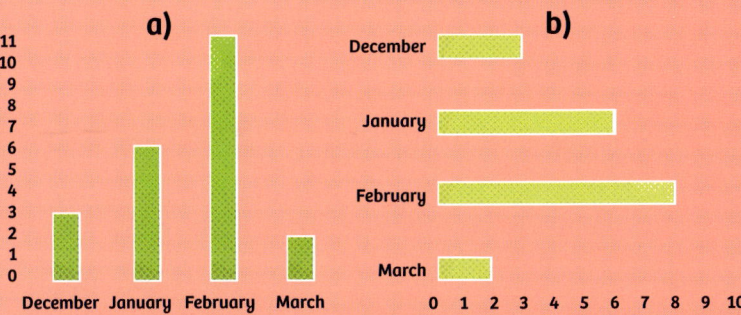

Students' favourite subject
English **12**   Maths **6**   Art **3**   History **3**

10 What angle on a pie chart represents the fraction $\frac{1}{4}$?

a) 45°   b) 90°   c) 180°

11 A thermometer reads a temperature of 20°C. Use the conversion chart to write down the temperature in °F.

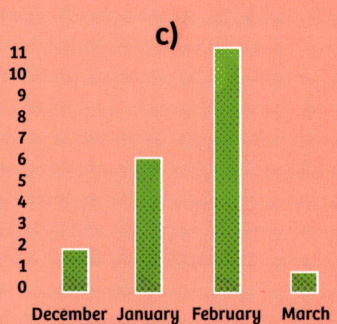

12 If the highest temperature across a period of 24 hours is 16°C and the lowest temperature is −2°C, what is the range of temperatures across that period?

45

13 A horizontal line on a time-distance graph shows that.

a) The object has stopped moving.
b) The object is slowing down.
c) The object is moving at a constant speed.

14 Korea Republic has a GDP of US$ 1,800 billion. Singapore has a GDP of US$ 400 billion. Korea Republic's population is 50 million. Singapore's population is 5.5 million. Which country has a higher GDP per capita?

15 What is the name for a survey of a country's entire population carried out by the government?

a) Sample   b) Average   c) Census

16 For a party, you have an entertainment budget of £70. If a magician costs £30 per hour (and can only be booked for full hours), how many hours can you afford to book her for? How much change will you have left over?

Green Hill	07:30am
Oxton	07:50am
Alton	08:00am
Brownside	08:10am
Gray's School	08:30am

17 Look at the school bus timetable to the left.

a) How long does the bus journey take in total?
b) If Jay catches the bus at Oxton, how long does his journey to school take?
c) Mara catches the bus at Brownside. How much later than Jay does Mara catch the bus?

18 The table for a four-team group stage of a football competition reads as follows with one match left to play. (Each team plays each other once. Three points are awarded for a win, one point for a draw.)

	P	W	D	L	Points	GD
China	3	1	2	0	5	+1
Canada	2	1	1	0	4	+2
England	2	1	0	1	3	+2
France	3	0	1	2	1	−5

a) Who will play in the final game?
b) What does the result of the final game need to be for England to win the group?
c) Can China win the group?

19 Fill in the missing numbers from this Major League Baseball table. *(Each team played 162 matches.)*

	W	L	%
Boston Red Sox	100	62	61.7
New York Yankees	98	64	60.5
Toronto Blue Jays	81	81	a)
Baltimore Orioles	b)	82	48.4
Tampa Bay Rays	62	c)	38.3

20 This can of tomato soup has the nutrition per 100g shown in the side.

a) If a whole can weighs 400 grammes, how many grammes of fat does it contain?

b) How many kcal of energy does a whole can contain?

c) How many grammes of salt does half a can contain?

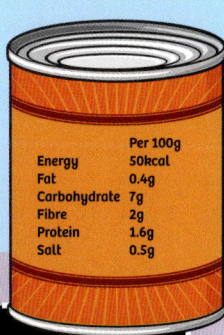

Per 100g
Energy 50kcal
Fat 0.4g
Carbohydrate 7g
Fibre 2g
Protein 1.6g
Salt 0.5g

Answers

QUIZ

1. a)
2. 15
3. b)
4. b)
5. c)
6. a) 18 b) 17 c) 50
7. a) Strawberry, 6 b) 3 c) 14
8. a)
9. b)
10. b)
11. 68°F
12. 18°C
13. a)
14. Singapore
15. c)
16. You can book the magician for 2 hours. You will have £10 change.
17. a) 1 hour b) 40 minutes c) 20 minutes
18. a) The final game is between Canada and England.
b) England need to win the game by any scoreline to win the group.
c) China cannot win the group.
19. a) 50 b) 80 c) 100
20. a) 1.6g b) 200kcal c) 1g

FROM THE BOOK

Page 7 Leon is exactly the mean height.

Page 13 35 people bought coffee on Tuesday.
a) 13 Children prefer pepperoni.
b) More children prefer meat or seafood over vegetables.
c) You will need five pizza symbols for mushrooms: four whole pizzas and one half pizza.

Page 15 1. Brazil has won the World Cup the most times.
2. 13 countries have made the final.
3. The Netherlands has made the final three times and lost on each occasion.

Page 17 a) 90° b) Half of the children prefer football. c) 4 children prefer netball.

Page 18 The cycle ride is 3.2 kilometres.

Page 19 The toy car costs 63 Yuan. The cat weighs 10 pounds.

Page 22 The women's record has improved the most.

Page 23 Kai took the bus to school. He went swimming at 11am. He arrived at Niall's house at 3.20pm.

Page 33 a) Science b) English c) Sport

Page 37 a) Canada cannot qualify.
b) France and China just need to draw their final matches to qualify.
c) For Nigeria to qualify with a draw, Canada need to beat China.

Page 40 Five full cans of beans provide 2,000 calories.

Page 41 As one example, you could choose a baked potato, a portion of carrots and two boiled eggs.

Page 42 If you want to go skiing, you should visit in November, December, January, February or March.

Index

100 metres world record 22

aces (tennis) 6

bar charts 14–15
baseball 6, 37
BMI (Body Mass Index) 34
budgets 28–29
buildings, tallest 22
bus timetable 32

carbohydrates 40
carbon dioxide 27
censuses 20–21
Chinese tallies 8
cities as destinations 43
clean energy 27
climate change 26–27
climograph 42
coffee shop 13
conversion graphs 18–19

data 4
diabetes 40
Domesday book 21
dot plots 10–11

election results 11
English Premier League 36
exam timetables 33
exercise 34

FIFA World Cup 15
film ratings 12
fitness, measuring 34–35, 38–39
flea jumping 30
football 36, 37, 38–39
fossil fuels 27

GDP 31
global warming 26–27
GPS trackers 38
greenhouse gases 27

health, measuring 34–35
heart rate 35
heat map 38–39
heights 7
Hockey Stick graph 26
holidays 42–43

league tables 36–37

Major League Baseball (MLB) 37
mean 6
medals table 15
Messi, Lionel 38

nutrition 40–41

parliament 11
percentage wins 37
pictograms 12–13
pie charts 16–17
presentations 17

range 30

school timetables 33
smart watches 35

tallies 8–9
temperature 19, 24, 25, 26
tennis 6
tides 24
time graphs 22–23
timetables 32–33
thermometers 19
Tukey, John 9
Tukey tallies 9

vitamins and minerals 41
Voyager 2 23

weather data 24–25

yo-yo test 38–39

zoo visit 12